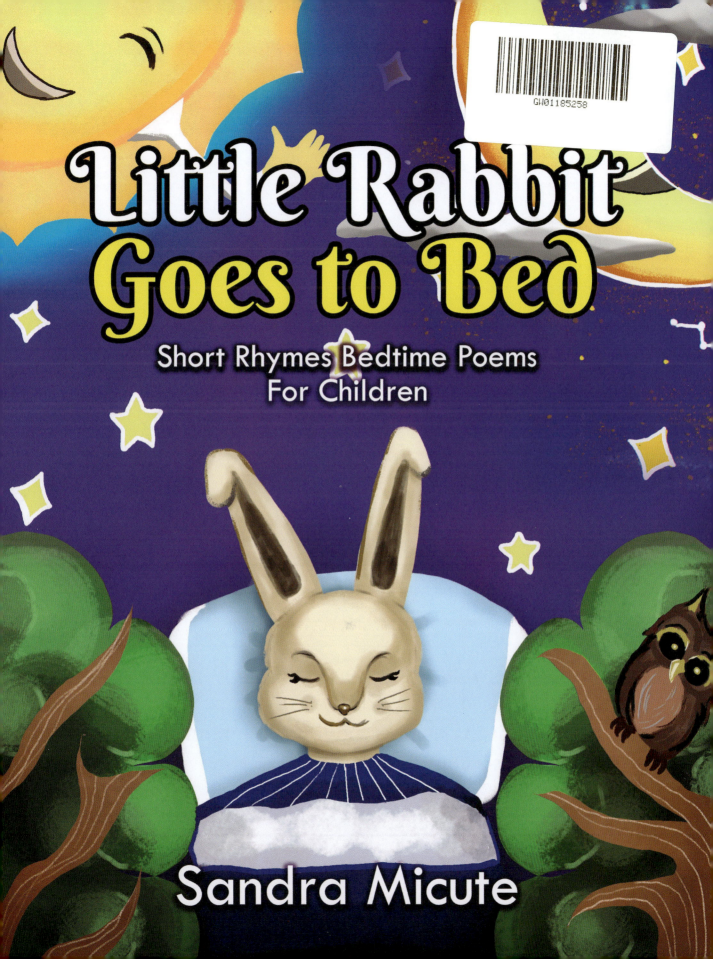

Copyright © 2022 by Sandra Micute - All rights reserved

No part of this publication or information in it may be quoted from or reproduced in any form or by means such as printing, scanning, photocopying or otherwise without prior written permission from a copyright owner.

Illustrated by: Cyan Avogadoyle

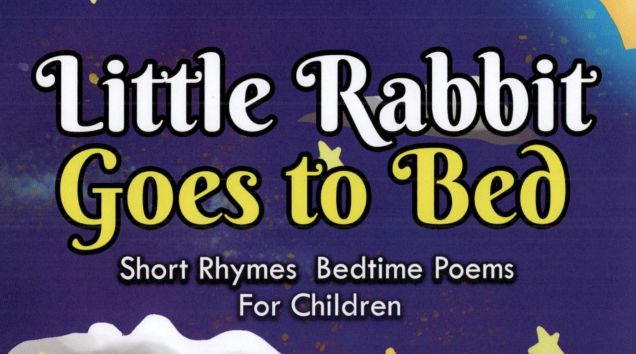

Little Rabbit Goes to Bed

Short Rhymes Bedtime Poems For Children

Sandra Micute

Early evening yet again
All the animals go to bed.
One little rabbit can't fall asleep
Tip tap, a lullaby is coming to help.

Bring for this cute rabbit
A soft pillow of sweet dreams.
Draw a pretty flower on a window
For its eyes to see.

Climb oh big mountain
To reach a tall sky.
Shine oh white moon
For our rabbit to smile.

Sing a sweet song
Lullaby, lullaby.
Bring beautiful dreams
For the rabbit tonight.

Little cloud, little cloud
Please show me the moon.
So during the dark night
It can shine through my window.

- Maybe I will and maybe I won't, -
The little cloud laughed.
- But what will I get
If I do what you asked.

I can share you my poem
I can sing you my song.
You won't be left alone
Until we both fall asleep.

- That sounds very nice
And I will get a new friend.
The moon will shine bright
And will wish us goodnight.

Spring sunny spring,
Oh, where are you?
Show yourself quick
Bring warmth with you.

I looked all day
And I looked all night.
Where oh where,
Did you manage to hide?

Like night changes day
So seasons change way.
Spring comes after winter
To brighten the day.

The sun smiles so warmly
And moon swings with joy.
We play during day time
Then sleep until dawn.

Calm, warm evening
What will you bring me?
What do you carry
In your bag of secrets?

A pillow full of laughter.
A blanket full of dreams.
On tip toes so quietly
A night is sneaking in.

Softly close the room doors
Where the little one sleeps.
Carefully cover their bedsheet
To have the dreams so sweet.

While the bright stars sparkle
High up in the sky.
The big, happy moon
Will watch over you all night.

The trees and the sky
Were covered by moon's light.
I'm coming to bring you
A warm, starry night.

I walk without feet
And fly without wings.
I bring many dreams
With ribbons as gifts.

I color your dreams
In pink, blue and red.
And cover your sleep
With motherly love.

As you drift into sleep
To the land full of dreams.
I fly through the sky
Where the moonlight's so deep.

Little rabbit sweat all day
Busy, busy in the kitchen.
Work hard with his little paws
To bake tasty cakes for the children.

A friendly mouse came over
Curious about the sweet smell.
What could be so tasty
That the rabbit was baking?

- Hello my dear neighbor, -
The cute mouse spoke.
- Can you share a cake
For my babies at home?

- Of course, - said the rabbit.
- I baked enough for you to eat,
And for the little children
Before they go to sleep.

My child, oh my sweetheart
Please close your cute eyes.
The sun now has set
To rest for the night.

My child, oh my sweetheart
Please lay in the bed.
The moon through the window
Will smile through the night.

My child, oh my sweetheart
It's late and it's dark.
Let sweet, happy dreams
Arrive at your side.

My child, oh my sweetheart
Please rest through the night.
The morning will come
To say a big and loud 'Hi'.

One mischievous Evening
Was swinging on tall grass.
When it became late
It went looking for a bed.

When it saw a deep lake,
It decided to go for a swim.
It went down to the bottom
And laid down for some rest.

It was peaceful and quiet,
And it was about to fall asleep.
When two frogs cried out loud;
- What a shock! How can this be?

They were about to step in
And tell the Evening what they think.
But a fish that came by
Told the frogs to take a hike.

Sun was hopping
Through the clouds
Moon was chasing
With the stars.

Morning gasped,
Daylight cheered.
Evening clapped
For all to hear.

The day was fun
And things went well
But time passed fast
We all went to rest.

When you lay down
In a warm bed,
A sweet goodnight
Your mom will tell.

Little rabbit went to bed
Rabbit's mommy came to check.
Put your favorite pajamas on
Bed is waiting to keep you warm.

The play time's over
The day was long.
The evening is calling
For games to stop.

The trees and flowers
Are already asleep.
And all your friends
Will join you in dreams.

Little rabbit closed its eyes
Rabbit's mommy said goodnight.
Sweet dreams I wish you
Let my love be with you.

Once in a deep part of the forest
A wonderous thing has happened.
A wolf bored of being lonely
Decided to change its hide.

- I don't want to be
A grey wolf anymore,
I will change to brown
And will be a good guy more.

In the middle of a meadow
A brown wolf sat to eat.
Chewing on a green grass
The taste was bitter sweet.

Sun is laughing in the sky
Birds are chirping flying by.
Sometimes brown and sometimes grey,
Wolf is wolf is what they say.

Lullaby, Lullaby
Bring some sweet dreams.
So my baby, dear baby
Will fall fast asleep.

The stars will shine bright
Through the night in the sky.
The moon will keep watch
To prevent noise and harm.

The clouds soft and fluffy
Will keep you so warm.
The wind will swing cradle
So you sleep until dawn.

And when you awake
The sun will be up.
Your mommy will greet you
With smile full of love.

Printed in Great Britain
by Amazon